THAT HOW IT WAS

WOMEN IN THE WYCHWOODS DURING WORLD WAR TWO

WYCHWOODS
LOCAL HISTORY
SOCIETY

THE WYCHWOODS LOCAL HISTORY SOCIETY IS
GRATEFUL TO THE GREENING LAMBOURN TRUST FOR A
VERY GENEROUS GRANT TOWARDS THE COST OF
PUBLISHING THIS BOOK

FRONT COVER: Demonstrating the use of a stirrup hand pump,
from a cigarette card in a series of fifty air raid precautions produced
by WD & HO Wills.

BACK COVER: Watercolour by Ted Rawlins painted in about 1941,
with Rawlins shop on the left and Mrs Martin's cottage, where
Mary Barnes was first evacuated, behind the telegraph pole. The
kerb is marked to provide guidance during the blackout.

For further information about Wychwoods Local History Society
contact the secretary Wendy Pearse, Littlecott, Honeydale Farm,
Shipton under Wychwood, Oxfordshire OX7 6BJ

✢ ✢ ✢ ✢ ✢ ✢ ✢ ✢ ✢ ✢ ✢ ✢

Copyright © Wychwoods Local History Society 2000
ISBN 0 9523406 6 6
Produced & designed by Bibliofile of Chipping Norton 01993 830122
Printed by Clouds Hill Printers, Chipping Campden

✝ ✝ ✝ ✝ ✝ ✝ ✝ ✝ ✝ INTRODUCTION

Is it possible to capture a sense of what life was like in the Wychwoods during the Second World War? The area enjoyed moments of celebrity with the brief internment of the Mosleys at the Shaven Crown Inn and the presence of Christopher Fry's wife in a tiny rented cottage. However, the real 1939-1945 story rests in the memories of long time local residents. In the spring and summer of 1999 we asked women who spent at least part of the war period in Shipton under Wychwood, Milton under Wychwood and Ascott under Wychwood, and who still live locally, to talk to us about their recollections. With their willing co-operation, we also tape-recorded the conversations and then transcribed them so that afterwards we could study what was said. For several, memory extended back well before 1939, and for Rose Burson, aged 99, the First World War seemed as vivid as the Second and 'much worse', because members of the family were killed: 'I lost a brother, I lost two brothers-in-law'.

It is more than 60 years since the declaration of war on 3 September 1939, and memory is a fragile witness, inevitably affected by later experience. People have read about war-time and seen films about it – some historic, some reconstructions. They are also each day made aware of scenes from all over the world. As Vi Smith, aged 89, reflected 'Television puts everything else behind, doesn't it?' This comment sums up well how our viewpoints are formed by the media.

The simplest and most spontaneous memories were perhaps the most graphic. Looking back, people's impressions were often of the 30s and 40s in general, rather than specifically the war years. Rationing did not end with VE day or VJ day. But common themes emerged, giving us confidence in the general coherence of our picture. In what follows we have used people's own words and have identified the speakers by their initials. We also used notes made of an interview with Mrs Winifred Dolton who died in 1994 and a letter from Mrs Brenda Bishop who now lives in the USA, and for background information, the minute books of the Wychwood Women's Institute and the Shipton and Milton Comforts Fund and the log books of Shipton and Milton village schools.

We thank all those who joined in this oral history project, and all who helped us prepare the material for publication, particularly Sue Richards.

ANTHEA JONES, SUE JOURDAN, JOHN RAWLINS, JANET WALLACE & TRUDY YATES

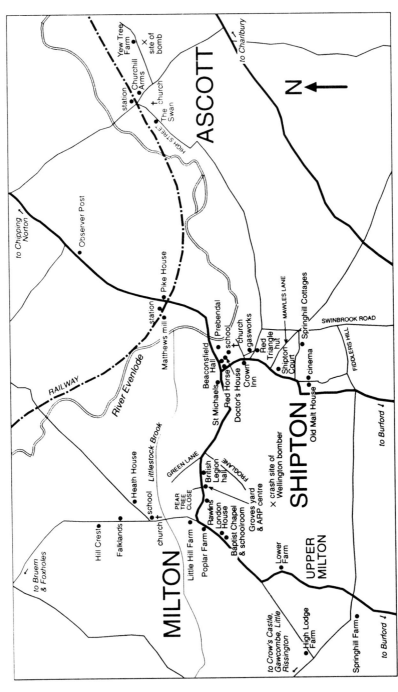

MAP OF THE WYCHWOOD VILLAGES SHOWING THE PLACES REFERRED TO IN THE TEXT

✝ ✝ ✝ ✝ ✝ ✝ ✝ WYCHWOOD WOMEN

Brief biographies of those who gave us a general view of life in the Wychwoods 1939–45 are included here. Others who have given help in particular areas are described in the text. Married names have been used throughout.

MARY BARNES née Bond (MB) Mary was born in Canning Town, London on 23 September 1927. She came to the Wychwoods on 1 September 1939 having been evacuated with many other children from London. She was first billeted with Mrs Martin who had a hairdresser's shop (next to Rawlins' video shop) and then she moved to Mr & Mrs Ivor Timms at 8 Pear Tree Close, Milton. Her mother eventually came from London to live in Fiddlers Hill, Shipton, and Mary moved there later. She worked firstly at Shipton Court Farm and then at Shipton Stores. She married Les Barnes in June 1945 at St Mary the Virgin Church, Shipton and lived for several years in Swinbrook Road, later moving to Upper High Street. They had four children.

ROSE BURSON née Barnes (RB) Rose was born on 18 May 1900 on an estate at Eastwood Hay, at Westwood Hay, near Newbury where her father was head gamekeeper for 47 years. There were 14 children in the Barnes family. Rose was number 12 and, from the moment she could walk, she was her father's little helper. Her happiest memories are of assisting him with the nest boxes, pheasant eggs and young birds. Although her ambition was to be a teacher, she was so touched when she saw a convoy of wounded soldiers at Reading in the First World War that she immediately signed up for the Land Army. After several postings she ended up in Milton in 1917. When the war was over, she became a permanent Milton resident when she met and married Stan Burson. Their daughter Kathleen was born in 1924 and their son Michael, recently chairman of Milton Parish Council, was born in 1944 – the surprise of the century, as Rose puts it. She has lived through and can vividly recall every year of the 20th century.

VALERIE DAVIS née Timms (VD) and PETER DAVIS (PD)   Valerie was born on 28 May 1933 at 8 Pear Tree Close, Milton under Wychwood. Her father, Ivor, came from Chadlington daily to work as a carpenter at

Alfred Groves & Sons and had met his wife Rose from Abingdon while working at Boars Hill, Oxford. After their marriage they moved into a newly built house in Pear Tree Close. It was here that Valerie and her brother were born and where she stayed until her marriage to Peter Davis, whose father and mother lived at the Old Malt House, Shipton. Mr Davis had a large milk-round, while Mrs Davis first worked at and then owned Dangerfields, London House, Milton, which was an outfitters and drapers, and also housed a small library. Valerie attended the primary school in Milton and was later awarded a scholarship to Burford Grammar School. Peter also contributed to the interview.

DAPHNE EDGINTON née Rose (DE)   Daphne was born on 29 September 1921 at Kingham. She was the fourth of six children of Tom and Lilian Rose, who farmed at Churchill Heath. Daphne married Bryan Edginton and came to the Wychwoods in 1940 'one day *before* my nineteenth birthday and one day *after* the harvest was in.' The Edgintons farmed at Crow's Castle at the extremity of Milton parish by the Gloucestershire border, where Daphne bore her two children, cooked for Italian and German prisoners of war, plucked poultry, skinned rabbits, made her own and her childrens' clothes, nursed baby lambs in the kitchen, cooked for the haymakers and the threshers, sold 60 dozen eggs a week and shot pigeons in the winter.

JOAN HALL née Slatter (JH)   Joan Hall was born in a cottage at the back of the Red Horse in Shipton and was nineteen years old on the day that war broke out. One of nine children, she lived at home to keep house for her father, a signalman at Bruern, after her mother had died. Joan

volunteered to work in the war-time canteen run by Dr Scott in the YMCA Red Triangle hut. She married Jim in May 1941 and he left that afternoon for service with the RAF in South East Asia. They did not see each other for four and a half years, but wrote to each other every day, the letters often arriving in bundles. At one point Joan did not hear from Jim for six months. They now live in Coombes Close, Shipton and Jim contributed to the interview.

MARJORIE RATHBONE née Bolton (MR)   Marjorie was born in Nottingham in 1912 and moved to Loughborough for six years before coming to the Wychwoods in 1927 where her family lived at 1 Shipton Road, Milton. Her father, Ted, was chief engineer at Alfred Groves and Sons on the opposite side of the road. Later, Marjorie too went to work for Groves in the office until 1938 when she married Geoff Rathbone, another Groves' employee. Their home, Sherwood in Frog Lane, had been built the year before. In 1939, Marjorie gave birth to their first child, Peter, nine days after the outbreak of war. The rest of the war was spent bringing up her family, later increased by a daughter, sorting out evacuees, much WI work and regularly collecting for National Savings and the Red Cross. Marjorie and her son still live in Sherwood.

BETTY SCOTT née Fullerton (BS)   Betty was born at Bedford Park near Chiswick on 27 January 1913. She started training to become a nurse at Harrow Hospital and it was there she met her husband, Dr Gordon Scott. After a few years of accompanying him while he furthered his career, they came from London in 1936 to start work at Shipton in general medical

practice in the Wychwoods. They moved into Nara now known as The Doctor's House, with a small surgery attached. Besides bringing up four children, Betty had to help out in many ways as the practice was single-handed, looking after the telephone and dealing with emergencies. Her eldest daughter Janet Wallace (JW) also contributed her memories as a wartime schoolgirl.

VI SMITH née Miles (VS), and Barbara and Colin Pearce (BP and CP)   Vi Smith was born in Shipton on 19 March 1910 in the cottage that is the lefthand side of the house now called Winterseeds. About a year later her parents moved to 9 High Street, Shipton, where she lived until she was married in 1932. Her husband was a clerk at Matthew's flour mill. Her first married home was along Meadow Lane at Littlestock, and that was where her daughter Barbara was born. 'I didn't have electricity when I was first married, we had an oil lamp'. Then she moved to a new bungalow, Falklands in Bruern Road, Milton, where she was in 1939. The Tripps were billeted on her there. When the manager of Matthew's mill died, in 1940, her husband took his place and they moved to Pike House, which went with the job. The house, which has since been extended, was cold and difficult to keep clean because 'it was right on the railway'. Hot water was heated in a copper with a fire underneath. 'My husband always lit the fire before he went to work'.

Barbara went to Shipton Church of England school and then to Burford Grammar School. Clothes rationing was still in force, and it was difficult to get enough coupons to buy the required school uniform. She used to come from school to visit her grandmother at 9 High Street, 'and then Gran would say "Shall we go and get some tomatoes?" or whatever. You could go to Shipton Court in the gardens, into the kitchen gardens and get your hot tomatoes out of the greenhouse – I used to go and do that – and lettuce – they grew a lot of things like that, and that must have been during the war – I was only a little girl [when I] used to come here from school.' In 1958 she married Colin Pearce, son of the headmistress in Milton. The Pearces came to Milton in 1927 because Mrs Pearce got a job as a teacher; as a married women she was not allowed to teach in Wales, and her husband, who was a miner, was out of work. Two years later Mrs Pearce became the head of Milton school and moved into the School House. Colin was born in 1933. Mrs Pearce was a strict disciplinarian and much respected in the area. Barbara was alarmed at first when she went with Colin to meet her. Now Barbara and Colin live in 9 High Street, her mother's old home, and Vi lives nearby in Bowerham. Colin also contributed to the interview.

MB Mary Barnes	VD Valerie Davis	CP Colin Pearce
BrB Brenda Bishop	WD Win Dolton	BS Betty Scott
BB Betty Brown	DE Daphne Edginton	VS Vi Smith
RB Rose Burson	JH Joan Hall	MR Marjorie Rathbone
IC Irene Carpenter	DH Dorothy Harrison	DT Dorothy Treweeke
PC Peggy Coombes	CM Cicely Miller	
PD Peter Davis	BP Barbara Pearce	

✝ ✝ ✝ ✝ ✝ ✝ ✝ ✝ ✝ ✝ ✝

Inevitably in a project like this with elderly interviewees deaths are likely to occur. Sadly Mary Barnes and Betty Scott both died before completion of this book.

DECLARATION OF WAR ✟ ✟ ✟ ✟ ✟ ✟

War was declared on 3 September 1939. Several of our interviewees vividly recalled that hot and sunny day.

"Declaration of War? I recall it very plainly. I was in the garden, and the window of the sitting room was open and I remember that when Chamberlain said that we were at war I looked through the window and said 'Oh good. Do you think that it will last long enough for me to get into the Air Force?' My mother, with tears rolling down her cheeks said, 'Dorothy, do you know what war means?' I can still hear her saying that. She had lived through the First World War. DH

"I was in church, we had come down with the school to Shipton Church, and I fainted. They brought me out and sat me on a seat in the vicarage garden and my teacher came out with me and they said war had been declared. So I remember that very well, sitting on a seat in the vicarage garden. MB

"I remember the day war was declared. I took the two evacuees to church and

during the service the radio was put through and it was announced at eleven o'clock. We came home to a roast beef lunch and our evacuees said that they could not eat it as they always had bread and jam, but, obviously, what they had heard in church must have upset them. CM

"I'd just taken Janet to church and we'd got home and we heard the sirens, so needless to say we dithered because we didn't know what to do and then we went outside to see if we could see any planes anywhere. BS

THE ARRIVAL OF TEACHERS AND CHILDREN FROM WEST HAM AT CHIPPING NORTON STATION ON 1 SEPTEMBER 1939, WITH THEIR GAS MASKS AND LABELS.

Evacuees had arrived in the Wychwoods even before the declaration of war, and for some years preparations had been made in anticipation. Every one talked about Hitler and the possibility of war.

" Everyone was talking about it quite a lot. What he was going to do and what he wasn't going to do and of course he never did what he was going to do and it went from there, didn't it, when he invaded Poland and the war started. RB

" We all thought Hitler was awful, such a cruel man and we were just sort of waiting for something to happen, and also of course I remember Neville Chamberlain coming back with his piece of paper saying 'Peace in our time', and breathed a sigh of relief but unfortunately it didn't succeed that way. BS

✝ ✝ ✝ ✝ THE ARRIVAL OF EVACUEES

The government had prepared for large scale evacuation of children from cities to safer country areas so billeting officers enlisted the help of Wychwood WI for billeting surveys of every house that could take in evacuees. In 1938 after Chamberlain's return from Munich with the hope

of peace, these preparations were put on hold but by 1939 this hope had faded. The remaining gasmasks and civil defence leaflets were distributed by the WI who were again asked to carry out more billeting surveys.

"I helped to carry out the billeting survey. I did the area near High Lodge. I can't remember who gave the instructions or how the survey was done. MR

On 1 September 1939, two days before war was declared, the official evacuation of cities began. Mary Barnes aged 11 lived in London with her mother and father and two-year-old sister near the docks.

"I can remember a couple of weeks before the war we used to go to school prepared to go at any time. We had to take a packed lunch and parade round the playground everyday as if we were going then we would go back to lessons and wait for the day which came on 1 September. We said 'cheerio' to our mums every morning not knowing if we would be going home in the afternoon. Then, on 1 September, we were told that it was time for us to go, we were only going to be away a fortnight. We walked up the street in double file towards Upton Park station, a lot of the mums came and waved to us, some were crying. I can remember leaving school and going on a train and nobody knew where we were going and I remember we saw Windsor Castle in the distance. Whether the teachers knew where we were going they didn't let on, but we came to Chipping Norton [station] where there were a number of coaches waiting to meet us. We were taken to the Town Hall and given a carrier bag each, in which we had a tin of corned beef, a tin of Nestles milk, a bar of chocolate, some biscuits - I can't remember what else, this was to help out the people who we were going to stay with. I mean we hadn't a clue what was to happen, and there were some little tiny ones - five years old – as well.

We were taken to the Baptist schoolroom [in Milton], and I can remember looking round and seeing a number of sacks filled with straw or hay and I thought that this was where we were going to stay. But there were a lot of people there who took us off in ones and twos to meet our new families. I was first billeted with a Mrs Martin and she had a hairdressers – you know – Rawlins' shop. Then she fell pregnant and had a baby and of course there were two of us billeted with her. So they had to find us somewhere else to live and that was when we went over to Mrs Timms in Pear Tree Close. MB

The children sent here on that first official evacuation on 1 September all came from Upton Cross School, West Ham. Ascott school received at least 32 children and two teachers, Milton at least 86 children and seven

EVACUEES FROM WEST HAM AND DAGENHAM IN CALAIS FIELD, MILTON, WITH MISS CLARK, 1941. MARY BARNES IS FOURTH FROM LEFT IN THE BACK ROW.

teachers and Shipton at least 63 children and five teachers all of whom had to be found accommodation. They were met by the billeting officers who allocated suitable billets or foster-homes with the help of the Women's Institutes whose members were often also members of the Women's Voluntary Services for Civil Defence (WVS).

Valerie Davies aged 6 was waiting excitedly for the evacuees' arrival.

"I can remember waiting for all these children and the house had all been altered upstairs and the mattresses on the floor. And we had two school teachers [Miss Watts and Miss Willis] instead of children and I cried myself to sleep. It was not long after they moved to Mrs Phillips at the shop, and then we had Mary Bond and Olive Barker. Olive didn't stay long. I think her mother came down and took her home. I was six years younger than Mary, six years older than my brother and I was sort of on my own in the midst of it. I remember all the evacuees about in the village – there were those at the Tibbitts. They were part of our lives then, I suppose that we just accepted them. VD

Many evacuee family groups had to be split as most foster-homes used

VALERIE DAVIS (RIGHT) WITH MARY BARNES HOLDING RAYMOND, AND ANOTHER EVACUEE, OLIVE BARKER, PHOTOGRAPHED IN 1940.

were only small cottages which could only take a maximum of two. Billeting officers were anxious to avoid mixing the sexes (local and evacuated) so evacuated brothers and sisters were usually separated into different billets. If evacuated children had problems with their billet, they could make known their complaints and grievances to their own peers, siblings and teachers, or to the local WVS, teachers and doctor. Evacuees could, and did, contact their own parents. Complaints over billets ranged from homesickness, primitive conditions compared to their own homes, harsh discipline, and verbal, mental, and physical abuse by fosterparents. There were also complaints from fosterparents about the habits, manners and behaviour of the evacuees and their parents. Some changes of billet were found necessary. Billeting officers had to make sure that the correct fosterparents were receiving the correct billeting allowance for each evacuee; 10s 6d a week for the first evacuee child and 8s 6d for every subsequent child in 1939. These rates were later changed to make allowance for age. Five shillings was paid for each teacher accommodated. The duties of the billeting officer applied only to those officially evacuated by the local authorities and not to the military, war-workers nor to children and families who made their own evacuation arrangements, although it was not unknown for the billeting officer to help out. Billeting officers did have compulsory powers to impose official evacuees on households but it is thought that hereabouts it was mostly done by persuasion. Joan Hall commented 'Of course if you had evacuees it wasn't your choice. If you had a spare bed you had evacuees. That was a thing that we never came to terms with.'

Vi Smith took in the Tripps, a mother and her two children.

"They had a committee. All places had to have them and it was according to what accommodation you'd got what you could house and who you had. I was lucky in that I had nice people, you know, who weren't dirty or slovenly – very fortunate. But you see they had to go to school and made the schools more difficult but this one little girl was almost similar age to Barbara and you can imagine Barbara being the only little one, she treasured all ̗ r things so and Jennifer was a little bit rough. We often had words about who should have what. VS

How long did she stay with you?

"Well, they eventually decided they liked Milton and her husband was still in Ilford. Her husband used to come down and see them and then they decided they would try to rent a cottage in Milton to give them a bit more

independence and he could come down when he was able, so they rented a cottage in Milton High Street for a time. VS

But not everyone took in evacuees.

"I was going to have evacuees but they didn't come to me because I had my mother in law. RB

"As I was pregnant before war was declared we did not have any evacuees. Mrs Shephard, two doors away at Greenmount had two, Lily Garland and Betty Window. My

FOSTER MOTHER MRS TIBBITTS WITH GEORGE LANE AND JAMES SIMPSON FROM WEST HAM, 1939.

mother had two, William and Grace Phillips, although later the boy was exchanged for Joyce Phillips. MR

Although many evacuees returned to London during the period of the 'phoney war' between September 1939 and April 1940, fresh official evacuations followed the beginning of the Battle of Britain and the later bombing raids. These raids also brought many who made their own way here.

Cis Miller was at home helping her mother:

" After about four to six weeks, when we came home one day and found a big pile of suitcases on the doorstep. It turned out that many of Jim's family had found their way down here, dumped their things on the doorstep and gone off onto the Green. There was Gran, Auntie, and an uncle and his fiancée. It was with some difficulty that they were all fitted in. There were 14 of us and them in the house at one time. But it was so much of a problem that they had to find other accommodation on Fiddler's Hill in Shipton. Dad stayed in London but made frequent visits. In fact, both sets of parents made visits. CM

Mrs Win Dolton, who came to Shipton during the war, told her story which illustrates the sanctuary that the Wychwood villages offered, recorded before she died. On 7 October 1940 her life changed completely. The blitz on London began with the East End as the main target area. When the air-raid sirens sounded Win took shelter wherever she could – in the shelter in the garden or in a surface shelter if she was out shopping with her daughter – while her husband, Dave, was engaged in the gruesome task of rescue and demolition of bombed-out buildings. As the bombing intensified, and with her husband on duty, Win sought the company of others in the public shelters especially during the night raids. She often went with her daughter and a neighbour to an underground shelter at a nearby school. That night, 7 October, her neighbour came round early to say that the school shelter was already full of people who had been bombed out. So they all went to shelter at St Luke's Church. That night the school shelter received a direct hit. Win decided that her luck was running out.

The following morning, which was Margaret's third birthday, they left. She had heard of Shipton under Wychwood from other returned evacuees so she bought underground tickets to Paddington, but there was a daylight raid so they only got to Aldgate East. Above ground she managed to hire a taxi to take them to Paddington with her fare paid by an unknown lady. There was another hold-up for raids on Tower Hill but

GOVERNMENT EVACUATION SCHEME RECORDS.
UNACCOMPANIED CHILD.

Ref. No. *1773*

Christian Name(s) *Joan*   Surname (BLOCK LETTERS) *Watts.*

Male/Female   Date of Birth: DAY *13* MONTH *3* YEAR *32*

National Registration Identity No. *DZEZ 100 3.*

Date of Evacuation   *With official School party/Privately.*

RECEPTION AREA PARTICULARS.	EVACUATION AREA PARTICULARS

Billeting Authority *WANTAGE URBAN DIST...*

(a) Evacuation Authority *West Ham* (b) Recovery Authority *West Ham*

School Attended *Upton Cross (West Ham) Unit, Wantage C.E.*

School Attended (Name, Address & No) *Upton Cross. E. 13.*

Address of Billet *Greyhaven, Ickleton Road,*

Name and Address of Parent or Guardian *Mrs J. H. Watts. (mother)*
24, Belton Rd, E 7.

Name of Householder *Mrs Allder.*

FORM EV. 42   *Strike out whichever is inapplicable

OVER

THE IDENTITY NUMBER DZEZ SHOWS THAT JOAN WATTS HAD ORIGINALLY BEEN EVACUATED TO SHIPTON. SHE WAS THEN MOVED TO LAUNTON, BICESTER, RETURNED HOME TO WEST HAM AND RE-EVACUATED TO WANTAGE IN JUNE 1940.

she eventually reached Paddington to begin their train journey to Shipton. Margaret was given a halfcrown as a birthday present by a fellow passenger. Careful watch was kept on the now painted-over signs until they reached Shipton under Wychwood. She stepped out onto the platform in a place she had only heard about, with her marriage lines in a tin box in one hand and Margaret on her other arm. She carried Margaret into the village where they were given a meal by Sally and Cecil Viner in Church Street. Starting with nothing she set up home in a condemned house now called Shep's Cottage on Fiddler's Hill and was given 'bits and pieces' by family, friends and neighbours. She was later joined by her sons who had been evacuated elsewhere and eventually by her husband when he was released from demolition work. 'It was a Godsend coming down here'. She died in Shipton in 1994 and Margaret, now Mrs Hunt, is still in Shipton, living in Ballards Close.

Even when the evacuees got away from the bombing there was no escaping the sound of the many training planes in the skies over the Wychwoods.

"I had my cousin for a little while just to take her out of London because they were being bombed and she was getting very scared. But she wasn't classed as an evacuee as she was a relative, but she was terrified of the planes. I always remember how frightened she was – as soon as she heard a plane coming she got under a table and put the tablecloth over her, she was that frightened. She always thought they were going to drop a bomb as soon as she heard a plane. VS

At times it was difficult to find space for the evacuees and many moved several times within the village.

CERTIFICATES ISSUED AFTER THE END OF THE WAR. ON THE LEFT A CERTIFICATE SENT TO FOSTER MOTHERS SIGNED BY THE QUEEN, AND ON THE RIGHT ONE SENT TO SCHOOL CHILDREN SIGNED BY THE KING.

I WISH TO MARK, BY THIS PERSONAL MESSAGE, my appreciation of the service you have rendered to your Country in 1939.

In the early days of the War you opened your door to strangers who were in need of shelter, & offered to share your home with them.

I know that to this unselfish task you have sacrificed much of your own comfort, & that it could not have been achieved without the loyal co-operation of all in your household.

By your sympathy you have earned the gratitude of those to whom you have shown hospitality, & by your readiness to serve you have helped the State in a work of great value.

Mrs. K. Rawlins.

8th June, 1946

TO-DAY, AS WE CELEBRATE VICTORY, I send this personal message to you and all other boys and girls at school. For you have shared in the hardships and dangers of a total war and you have shared no less in the triumph of the Allied Nations.

I know you will always feel proud to belong to a country which was capable of such supreme effort; proud, too, of parents and elder brothers and sisters who by their courage, endurance and enterprise brought victory. May these qualities be yours as you grow up and join in the common effort to establish among the nations of the world unity and peace.

George R.I

"The Hawtins next door did not take any from the first evacuation, but they took Irene Harrendence from the second evacuation. When the bombing on London began on September 1940, Betty Window's mother and step-father left London as they were bombed out and they came to live with us. They stayed for about two years until Mrs Window was pregnant and they moved to two rooms with Mrs Pritchard in the laundry up the High Street. She gave birth to a two-pound baby. Before they moved to the laundry Mrs Woolf had put them up. She lived in the last of the three new houses in Frog Lane. Meantime, Mr Window's sister, Mrs Jenkins and her husband had also moved from London to Milton and they were put up by the Hawtins next door. Betty Window later moved to live with Bill Hedges in The Square. Mrs Coombes, up The Square, also took in two evacuated teachers from Dagenham, Miss Clark and Miss Willis. Geoff's brother Harry and his wife Annie also left London during the bombing and they came to Milton to live up the High Street. They later had an evacuee, Patricia Standing, billeted on them. MR

At the third evacuation in September 1940 when the London blitz started, there was a family of three boys whom the billeting officer had difficulty in placing. It is said they were trailed around by Miss Batt, the chairman of the local WVS, and finally ended up in Pear Tree Close. Here, Mrs Win Miles agreed to take the twins and Mrs Rose Timms the other brother – just for the night which turned out to be four years!

✝ ✝ ✝ ✝ ✝ ✝ ✝ ✝ ✝ ✝ SCHOOL TIME

During the war years Milton Council Primary School had the good fortune to have the same three teachers, who all lived in Milton, for the whole period, although there were constant changes of the evacuated staff. Shipton Church of England School was less fortunate and had many staff changes with different head teachers. In 1939 Shipton CE School was the only school in the Wychwoods to take children for the full elementary age range of five to fourteen years. Children from Ascott transferred to Shipton at eleven. Milton school children were bussed to Burford at eleven or, if the parents preferred a Church of England education, they transferred to Shipton. Access to Burford Grammar school was by payment of fees or by gaining a county scholarship.

Following the arrival of the first evacuees most schools were overcrowded, and all had poor conditions – no running hot water, primitive toilets, no blackout and little in the way of air-raid precautions such as shelters. Milton and Shipton schools had heating problems with their high vaulted roofs. There were coal shortages and there was difficulty in obtaining cleaners to light fires. Throughout the war years there were spells of icy weather when water froze in the taps and periods of thaw when the drains were blocked. Even when the schools were open they were still cold. In January 1941, Shipton school log book recorded 'School very cold, although good fires are burning. Temperature at 10am only 38 degrees F.'

When asked whether it was cold at school, Valerie Davis said 'It must have been, but there again, was it imagination?' Peter Davis added 'You dressed accordingly or hopefully you did anyway. There was the big tortoise stove in the big room with a guard round it.'

To cope with the evacuees, Shipton school obtained the use of the YMCA Red Triangle hut and the Beaconsfield Hall. But by October 1939 both had to be given up, the former as it was 'unsuitable, poor light and ventilation' and the hall because it was requisitioned by the military who also commandeered the cookery hut in the playground for use as a NAAFI canteen. In Milton the Baptist schoolroom and the British Legion Hall were obtained for use. The Milton and London children used these places alternately, desk work being taken at the school and oral work in the halls; the same regime was used at Shipton. Later that year use of the Legion hall was discontinued. Milton children and evacuated boys were taught at the school and evacuated infants and girls were taught in the Baptist schoolroom.

The first evacuated children, from Upton Cross School at West Ham, who came to Shipton were transferred after only four months to Launton village near Bicester. The reason given in the school logbook was 'unsuitable and unsanitary conditions pertaining to the old buildings'. Thereafter Shipton school received no official evacuees apart from those transferred from Ascott at 11, those who changed billets and 13 evacuees from East Ham in October 1940 who arrived in Shipton with their mothers. In Milton, 39 more children arrived from Dagenham in June 1940, with 20 more in September, along with ten from Lyneham, some of whom were also evacuees. At this time the Church Room was also brought into use as part of the school. All local schools also took in unofficially evacuated children. Like most children, Valerie Davis, Mary Barnes, Barbara Pearce and her husband, Colin, seemed to have just accepted the situation and remember good relations with the newcomers after initial settling down.

"I even remember when the class sizes went up considerably when the evacuees came, obviously. I think they were thought to be rather odd to start with but I mean I made some very good friends with evacuees. CP

"The evacuees were integrated with us. I can remember at Milton there were so many of us there, and with the evacuees' teachers going over to the church room. I mean there was the curtain down the middle of the big room. But you just got on with it. VD

"We just learned from the books that were provided and didn't feel there was any shortage, Mrs Pearce's word was the rule and that was it. VD

"I don't remember shortages of anything probably because my mum was headmistress and she was a pretty stern woman. She loved her job and she fought tooth and nail to get things for the school. CP

A PHOTOGRAPH OF THE 'GARDENERS' TAKEN AT SHIPTON CE SCHOOL TO COMMEMORATE THE SILVER JUBILEE OF KING GEORGE V IN 1935 WHEN PREPARATIONS WERE ALREADY BEING MADE FOR WAR. *Standing* (left to right): John Collett, Frank Dangerfield, Walter Barrett, Cyril Dangerfield with Mr Horne behind, Eric Wiggins, John Walton, Melvyn Eeles, Charles Smith, Alfred Fowler. *Kneeling*: George Harris, Kenneth Weston, Ken Masters and Leslie Barnes. *Sitting*: John Shirley.

Ken Masters wrote home from Italy on 15 September 1944: 'All bombs and gunfire out here. Oh to be home in Ascott'. Two days later Ken was killed at Morchiano and lies buried in the Commonwealth War Graves Cemetery at Corriano Ridge, Italy. Wally Barrett, Cyril Dangerfield, and Ken Wright were also to die on active service. John Collett was killed in a farming accident. Les Barnes married Mary Bond, one of the evacuees to Milton.

There was little enthusiasm for school meals when they could be remembered at all.

"I can remember school dinners. Mrs Hawcutt and Mrs Harry Smith used to do it, and it was always the same, except at some time there must have been some food parcels came to school and we had some chocolate rice and the headmistress said how wonderful it was and how grateful we should be, but it was really not very nice, but you were made to feel you'd got to eat it whether you... because it was good for you, but that was the whole policy, it was good for you. VD

"We didn't have school meals, I don't think, not at St Mary's [Shipton]. I used to go home for dinner because we lived at Pike House then and so I always went home for lunch. Although there was a kitchen but I think that was later. I don't know whether there was one when I was there, I can't remember if they did school dinners. I expect I was awkward and went home. BP

"We used to go to cookery, I can't remember where. Must have walked to Shipton; they had a hut along the side there. We used to knit socks and that sort of thing at school. I was there till I was 15 so we weren't like little children, we were like secondary school children but we didn't have exams or anything like that. They were very kind. MB

"They were all older teachers, looking back, they were when we went to Grammar School. There were no young men about and that was it. They got it into your brain and that was it. VD

PREPARING FOR WAR ✝ ✝ ✝ ✝ ✝ ✝ ✝

Preparations for war at home were being made well before 3 September 1939. The government was particularly fearful of poison gas attack and gas masks were issued to all households, an event particularly remembered by those of our interviewees who were school age in 1939, Valerie Davis and Mary Barnes.

"Oh I remember those, they stank. And for a long time we had to carry them about and had a little rexine box, was it? And my brother, he was born in March 1939. They had a massive old coach built pram and Mother used to carry this great big gas mask about. VD

"I remember having them because I remember the little babies having those 'mickey mouse' ones. They were horrible to wear, absolutely stifling. I can remember the first and second day and the siren went and everybody reached for their gas masks. MB

Firefighting provision was made. Rose Burson remembered 'We had buckets of sand, because we used to go firefighting. And then we used to have pumps and pump water'. Betty Scott remembered two fires very close to her, neither caused by the enemy. At that time the doctor's surgery was by the house in Church Path, Shipton and the school was opposite.

" We had stirrup pumps. And of course our own surgery went up in flames during the war. They were all voluntary firemen. You know what the wooden hut of the surgery was like, you could almost reach to the roof without ladders, and they hacked at the door with their little axes. They wanted a ladder and we had to lend them our rickety ladder.

The school was going to make a canteen in a wooden hut in the playground which they used for carpentry and domestic work for girls. And they cleared out all of that and brought an army canteen there. And they'd just got it beautifully stocked up and he'd got a tortoise stove there. He made it up while he went to have his dinner at the Red Horse, and during that time

DR GORDON SCOTT
WITH HIS WIFE BETTY
HOLDING PAULINE,
AND JANET, 1938.

the thing went up in flames and all the tins of beans and things went pop, pop, pop, and everybody kept ringing us up to say 'Are you safe down there? Would you like to come up here?' They thought it was guns going off. BS

First-aid lectures were held and Betty Scott was expected to use her medical training. 'I was supposed to be in our own surgery, head of first-aid workers there, then of course we all went to first-aid lectures in the Red Triangle hut, I think it was.'

The whole country had, to observe the blackout to avoid giving guidance to enemy bombers. One of the principal memories of our interviewees was the blackness at night with not a light allowed to show.

"Somebody came round and jumped on you immediately for showing a light and you shouldn't. It was very dark in the village, because there were no street lights and I always remember that it seemed as though the evenings were nothing because the people couldn't go around so they just stayed in doors. Very restricted really. VS

"Mother had special frames made for all the windows covered with curtain stuff. One night I was reading in bed with a light on, and a bit of light must have been showing through and one of the Wilks came by and shouted 'Put that light out!' Another time we were waiting at Shipton station at night when a train stopped and a voice called out from an open window, 'Can you please tell me where we are?' Everything was blacked out. BB

Betty Scott was the Girl Guide captain:

"I had to go over to Clanfield because the Commissioner lived there and she was giving lessons to new Guiders. You had to go after dark and in those days you had your headlights with only just a slit of light. It was very tricky going from here to Clanfield. I must have been a lot braver than I am now though only half as brave as most people. BS

During the war Groves' yard in Milton was the centre of the Civil Defence in the area, as it had the Wardens' Post, mobile fire pump and rescue services. It also served as the HQ for the Milton platoon of the Home Guard and the centre for WI fruit preservation. At the beginning of the war, the air-raid warning siren caused some alarm but as the warnings became more frequent they tended to be ignored.

"My father, Ted Bolton, was responsible for the sounding of the air-raid siren at Alfred Groves' yard. He was not on the phone but Mr Walker would get in contact with him somehow, as he, Mr Walker, was chief ARP Warden who got the messages about air-raids. Mr Walker said that my father was the only one who could out-talk his wife. MR

Dorothy Harrison remembered 'They sounded the siren for nothing. There was a siren in Ascott. It was kept at the Churchill Arms. It went on and off, and someone had to turn the handle to make it go'. And Brenda Bishop recalled how she was delivering milk from Mr Wells' dairy farm.

" The first air-raid warning scared me stiff, and I dashed back to Poplar Farm only to be met by a very stern Mr Wells, telling me to go ahead and deliver to the customers. At the time I thought he was unfeeling but later saw that it wise as we had to learn to cope. BrB

" The day after war was declared the siren went, over in the yard. I can recall my mother running upstairs with three gas masks, one round her neck and bringing the others up, Jeff's and mine, and the evacuees'. She thought that we were going to be gassed straight away. CM

Betty Brown was 12 years old when war was declared.

" We lived in The Square at the time, right in the corner, next to Lydiatt's. They were very deaf, so whenever the siren sounded, which was on the top of Groves' yard, I had to go round to tell them that the air-raid warning had gone. The first time we heard the siren we were all in bed. We all came downstairs and huddled under the kitchen table, except father. He stayed in bed, saying that if they wanted to kill him they could do it while he was in bed. After that we didn't worry about any air-raid warnings. BB

Very few families had proper shelters and, most like Joan Hall, remembered 'making a bolt for the kitchen table'. Similarly Cis Miller said 'we had a very big heavy table and we used to gather under the table with the evacuees and Mum. That's where we spent our time'.

" We had one in the garden for the three families, Shepard, Hawtin and ourselves. It was underground, it was lit and we went down steps into it. We went down there a few times, but as Geoff said 'we shall catch our death of cold down there'. MR

Although taking shelter was abandoned as the war progressed, there were at least 26 aerial attacks, mainly indiscriminate dropping of parachute mines, high explosives and incendiaries, within a ten-mile radius of Shipton church in 1940, with more in 1941. They were probably intended for local airfields and Leafield Radio Station. On 23 September 1940 there was a machine-gun attack and ten bombs dropped near the radio station as well as a string of six bombs on Ascott. One fell in the garden of Dorothy Harrison's home while she was working at the farm next door.

BOMB CRATER IN HIGH STREET, ASCOTT IN SEPTEMBER 1940. DOROTHY HARRISON'S MOTHER, MRS SIMMONDS, IS SECOND FROM LEFT, WITH YEW TREE FARMHOUSE BEHIND.

" It blew the side off the house of Mr Jack Young and blew away the outside toilet and a damson tree in the garden. At that time everything was rationed so very much. Hardly any sugar, and Jack Young's wife was making jam, and when the bomb hit the side of the house and blew the stove out, she didn't say 'Ooh look at my kitchen', but 'Damn, all that sugar saved up for jam'. She had her priorities right. They closed the High Street and when [my] Dad came home from work he was unable to get home. They told him that the house was damaged but nothing more. 'Bugger the house, how's my family' was his response. They were okay. DH

Janet Wallace left home for boarding school in Yorkshire at the beginning of January 1943 and recalled vividly what happened there when there was an air-raid.

" Warnings usually came at night which meant we had to get up quickly, put on dressing gown and slippers, take an eiderdown or rug and assemble in the front hall, given a small green cushion and told to settle down on the floor and try to sleep. One night we had three alerts. Although we were not bombed, there were plenty of places around that were badly hit. We had daily prayers and we used to assemble once or twice a week to take part in a Litany during which we prayed for named family members who were in the armed forces.

We had a large map of Europe on the wall indicating how the war was going. We had to wear school uniform but we were always cold in the winter. When travelling to and from school we had to take our gas masks, identity cards and ration books with us always. Trains were always very full with civilians and troops, all train windows had some sort of lattice glued onto them. When peace was declared I was returning to school, but stayed overnight in London and enjoyed their bonfire and fireworks celebrations. JW

✝ ✝ ✝ ✝ ✝ ✝   SOLDIERS AND AIRMEN

It was not only children who were billeted on the villagers of the Wychwoods; the military billeted officers and NCOs in private homes and requisitioned any empty buildings. The 50th Northumbrian Division arrived in October 1939. They took over the Beaconsfield Hall, St Michael's Home, parts of Shipton Court and the Prebendal, the clubrooms of the public houses as well as barns, stables and their lofts. During their stay here that first winter, many were invited into local homes for tea or Sunday lunch, or merely to sit by the fire and chat; a practice that continued with later military arrivals.

Peter Davis remembered that they had three or four officers at the Old Malt House in Shipton, which fortunately had two staircases. 'It was divided off to a certain extent, the soldiers had the bottom end and we had Kethero's end. They had the front door and we had the back door.'

The 50th Division left to join the British Expeditionary Force in France in January 1940 and was later evacuated through Dunkirk at the end of May, although not returning to this area. The WVS were on hand at local stations where troop trains had priority on local lines but hospital trains had top priority. Dorothy Harrison remarked, 'At last people realised how serious the war was. I don't think that anyone did till then'.

Many of the evacuated soldiers were encamped in this area while they were reorganised. The Brigade of Guards used all previously requisitioned properties and more besides. Betty Scott recalled that they were under tents at Bruern Abbey while Joan Hall remembered that there was not a blade of grass left showing for the number of tents pitched on Shipton green, the verges and Dr Scott's orchard. They also encamped on Milton Green. Valerie and Peter Davis recalled 'the trenches on the Green because they weren't filled in for ages. I think it was when they were collecting everybody together'. And Betty Brown remembered 'the barn on the High Street, belonging to Mr Wells. The doors on the street were opened and they cooked in there. They always seemed to be cooking eggs. I suppose I must have been waiting for the school bus.' Dorothy Harrison recalled soldiers standing in the pouring rain on Ascott village green eating their meals at a field kitchen with a groundsheet over them.

Later, other divisions of the army were billeted in this area for training and manoeuvres prior to posting overseas. Betty Scott remembered them at the Beaconsfield Hall.

" They took over the village hall and I know they burned most of the chairs to make a fire to keep themselves warm. And I know the Dentistry Corps came down because when my sister who was evacuated to me, came with her two children, she was walking down Shipton High Street and coming towards her were two officers in uniform and they were both dentists she'd been to. And they used to come round and have a meal occasionally with us. They said they were so cold up there that the water froze in the hotwater-bottles – they had those china ones, where they were billeted at the Red Horse. BS

Dorothy Harrison remembered the Pioneer Corps who were billeted in the club-rooms of the two Ascott pubs, the Swan and the Churchill.

" They were in the station yard at Ascott at the end of 1941. You were not allowed in there. The Pioneers were stacking coal in great stacks and army lorries came in to collect. Then, eventually they went from coal to bombs, stacking them in piles alongside the roads. DH

The Pioneers also laid out bases for the US camp in the grounds of Bruern Abbey which by late 1942 were occupied by the 377th Airborne Engineers Battalion. Other Americans occupied St Michael's and parts of Shipton Court while they piled up dumps of ammunitions on the grass verges that were wide enough.

Peter Davis remembered the advantages of the American GIs.

" [There were] military police across the road and the Americans up at Bruern. I know I went up there often and they used to save us a piece of chocolate pie or whatever and always gave it to us. [I] met Philip Hackling coming back and he'd got a 25lb tin of pineapple chunks and we all had a dive-in and a handful – that was marvellous that was. Used to creep in and watch the films because they had film shows. PD

MT SECTION (NO 8 MU) AT RAF LITTLE RISSINGTON IN 1945 WITH BRENDA BISHOP LEFT
FRONT ROW. DOROTHY HARRISON'S FATHER, MR SIMMONDS, SECOND FROM RIGHT IN BACK ROW.

"I can remember the time when the coloured American got stabbed at the top
of Pear Tree Close one Saturday night. VD

With the approach of D-Day in 1944, the many dumps of munitions
were moved south towards the invasion ports and the people of the
Wychwoods got their grass verges back.

As well as the British and American soldiers in the Wychwoods, by
1945 there were more than 30 RAF airfields or landing grounds within a
20-mile radius of Shipton church. Most of them were for the training of
aircrew, by day and by night. By mid-1940 RAF Little Rissington alone
had 400 aircraft with another 170 at No 8 Maintenance Unit (also at
Little Rissington). With so many men under training perhaps it was
inevitable that there were accidents, some fatal. Many of our interviewees
recalled the crash of the Wellington bomber BJ728 in September 1942.
Betty Scott recalled that her husband was called out 'to the field at the
end of Frog Lane and when he got there, there was nobody to be seen and
then this airmen was found walking round in a rather dazed condition'.
He was the only survivor of the crew of five. On another occasion, Betty
Scott again,' There was a nasty one up by the station, and poor father had
to go up and see if he could render any assistance, but I fear the bodies
were blown to pieces. It crashed into the ground and set fire.'

SKETCH OF POST Y.I. BY HOPE BOURNE FROM THE WYCHWOOD WOMEN'S INSTITUTE BOOKLET
MILTON AND SHIPTON DURING THE WAR.

Ascott, Milton and Shipton each had their own Home Guard platoons, so, from 1940, mothers and wives had to put up with the absence of their menfolk who were called for duty in out-of-work hours. Lectures, training, exercises and parades had to be attended in evenings and weekends. Sometimes this involved all night guard duties at danger spots like railway bridges, road junctions and Leafield radio station.

" Well, my father got shot when he was in the Home Guard with a blank. They used to use – you know where Vi used to live in the Elms Cottage, that was derelict then, well, I think the WI used to make jam and things in there, but they did it for exercise with the Home Guard and somebody shot a blank at my father's face. That was a bit of a kerfuffle, I mean, luckily, it didn't hurt his eyes. VD

As well as the Home Guard some wives from the three villages had to contend with their husband's duty at the Observer Corps Post Y1 on the Chipping Norton road (where the present relay mast is situated). Operating a shift system, this post maintained a 24-hour watch from August 1939 for the next five and a half years, monitoring and identifying all aircraft in the skies over the Wychwoods.

FOR THE COMMON CAUSE ✝ ✝ ✝ ✝

Voluntary organisations took on important roles during the war with everyone doing what they could in their spare time. Many women were members of Wychwood Women's Institute, Women's Voluntary Service, the Red Cross, Mothers' Union, Shipton and Milton Comforts Fund, Wychwood Ambulance and National Savings. They were also involved in churches and chapels, British Legion, Girl Guides, Boys Brigade, Wychwood Players and the canteen in Shipton. And everyone knitted.

The Wychwood Women's Institute seemed to have been the mainstay of activities in Shipton and Milton. Cis Miller, Brenda Bishop, Daphne Edginton, Marjorie Rathbone and Rose Burson all belonged. Members knitted, collected salvage, made pyjamas for our prisoners of war and endlessly collected money for refugees and prisoners. They responded generously to appeals from, among many others, Burford Cottage Hospital, St Dunstan's Home for the Blind, National Children's Home, Queen Charlotte's Maternity Hospital and Great Ormond Street Hospital, the Red Cross, the Wychwood Ambulance and the Empire Cancer Campaign. They helped at the War Nursery at Bruern Abbey and made toys for the babies. They made lavender bags for London hospitals and air raid victims. They visited evacuees to 'report on necessitous cases'; entertained refugees, soldiers and evacuated children and their mothers;

TWENTY-FOUR UNDER FIVES FROM THE EAST END OF LONDON WERE CARED FOR IN A WAR NURSERY IN PART OF BRUERN ABBEY. THIS PHOTO WAS TAKEN IN ABOUT 1940.

SHIPTON AND MILTON
WARSHIP WEEK

Auction Sale

at

MILTON - UNDER - WYCHWOOD

in the

Joiners' Shop, Groves' Yard,

on

Saturday, March 28th, 1942,
at 2-30 p.m.

Very Valuable
DRESDEN CHINA
Paisley Shawls, Gold Coins, etc.,
will be sold.

On View Friday Afternoon
from 2-30 p.m. till 7 p.m.

Admission to view — One 6d. Savings Stamp.

W. T. PREECE & SONS, PRINTERS, MILTON-UNDER-WYCHWOOD, OXFORD.

POSTER FOR ONE OF THE ANNUAL WAR SAVINGS WEEKS HELD THROUGHOUT CHIPPING NORTON RURAL DISTRICT. MRS SCOTT REMEMBERED 'It seemed to me every time there was a war [savings] week, I was in the hospital having a baby.'

distributed ration books; held numerous sales of work and whist drives; and ran a poultry club and a regular produce stall of vegetables from members' gardens. In 1943 they were relieved to hear that they were not required to make camouflage nets. They also ran a preservation centre in the ARP room in Groves' yard particularly worked in by the ladies from across the road in Pear Tree Close — Valerie Davis' mother, Mrs Timms, Mrs Miles and Mrs Gee. The WI minutes for October 1941 record that 240lbs of jam had been made for sale and that it was intended to make chutney and rosehip syrup. The 12s 4d received for the hips already picked and dispatched would be given to the Russian Red Cross. The following autumn it was recorded that 118lbs of rosehips were dispatched for processing and 165lbs of jam made.

Daphne Edginton owned a canning machine that was used for canning sessions with the neighbouring WIs.

" Plums, there was quite an abundance of plums one year and we did canning and tons and tons of apples one year and we peeled and peeled and peeled and then we canned them. Some at Ascott, some at Chadlington, because they had got facilities. About half a dozen of us. It took quite a few because you've the peeling, and the canning and the sealing of the cans and the boiling and you had to time the boiling properly. And you had to write on them what they were [with a] special pen or dark coloured pencil. Very difficult. They went to a special place; it was all for the common cause in aid of the war effort. So they went off where they needed them, [to] canteens. DE

AIRGRAPH FROM MILTON AND SHIPTON
COMFORTS FUND WRITTEN BY MRS
FAIRBAIRN. THE LETTERS WERE
PHOTOGRAPHED AND ONLY THE FILM SENT
ABROAD. ORIGINAL 4 X 5 INCHES, 1944.

Wychwood WI meetings often had to be reorganised because of air-raids warnings, and the problems of meeting during the blackout in winter and the requisitioning of public rooms in the villages by the military or other organisations. Many talks gave advice on war-time problems: 'Meatless Meals' and 'Drying Dandelions Roots, Foxglove Leaves and Nettles' and 'Knitting with Unravelled Wool'. At some meetings they had cakes and biscuits but no tea and at others no refreshments at all, feeling it their patriotic duty to go without.

As well as all the hard work done by Wychwood WI, a huge amount was achieved by the Shipton and Milton Comforts Fund, often the same ladies. In early 1940 the Wychwoods Keep Fit Club – all women – ran a very successful social and it was decided to send some of the money raised to The Comforts Club inaugurated by the *Oxford Mail* to send 'little extras' to Oxfordshire persons serving in HM Forces. Dr Scott suggested that there should be a local fund and so commenced the Shipton and Milton Comforts Fund. (Ascott and Lyneham had their own funds).

At the beginning of the war, willing knitters had been found to send knitted comforts. By mid-1940 the Fund was able to send to over forty serving personnel a parcel containing a pair of socks, ten cigarettes and a quarter pound bar of chocolate together with a covering letter written by a member of the committee and a stamped addressed envelope for future requests. The money was raised from socials, weekly whist drives, dances and, by 1943, a pantomime in what had become designated each February as Comforts Week. In 1941 the committee of the Comforts Fund comprised five women with Mr Fairbairn as chairman, but it was Mrs Freda Fairbairn as secretary who was the one who ran the whole effort. Meetings were held in her house on the corner of Green Lane as well as the rehearsals of the pantomimes that she produced and for which she provided the musical accompaniment. She was also an active member of the WI.

By 1941 rationing, the cost of postage and other demands on local knitters had made it more difficult to send parcels so money was sent instead. Ten shillings was sent in May 1941 and £1 and 20 cigarettes at Christmas to all those serving in the British Isles together with a covering letter. Those serving abroad were credited with the amount in a Post Office account. Mrs Fairbairn noted from the replies received '[the money] appeared to come in the nick of time, just as they were completely broke'. Letters were also sent to relatives of those who died on active service together with £5 for needy cases together with any outstanding credits. Throughout the rest of the war members of the forces received letters and money from the Wychwoods. In August 1944 weekly parcels of biscuits, chocolate, a magazine, 40 cigarettes, matches, razor blades and stamps to the total value of eight shillings were sent to those in hospital; not easy with rationing and shortages. For Christmas 1944 £1 was dispatched to those serving in this country, letters to those in Europe and airgraphs to those elsewhere. With over 120 letters to write and another Comforts Fund Week to prepare, it was agreed that each member of the committee should write at least ten letters. Not quite as easy as it sounds

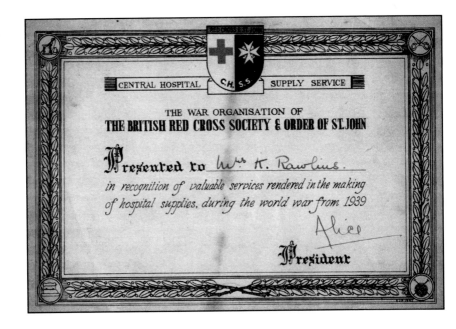

with time spent trying to keep up-to-date with the addresses of forces constantly on the move, buying the correct value postal-orders and crediting between 40 and 50 post office saving books, as well as all the demands of family and home in those days before domestic appliances.

At the end of the war with a substantial amount still in the Fund, it was agreed to give £5 to any member of the armed forces who had served five years and £1 for each year of service to the others, with any remaining balance divided equally between the prisoners of war. It appears from the Comfort Fund minute book that 166 recipients of this share-out received amounts varying from one shilling and sixpence to £8 15s. And at the end all that was left was the £5 invested by the ladies of the Wychwoods Keep Fit Club.

As if the WI and Comforts Fund were not enough work, many also raised money for the Red Cross and collected for National Savings. Rose Burson recalled 'We did a lot of Red Cross work. We formed a Red Cross Committee, six of us. I was always making toys. I was soaking felt hats in a bucket of water, then I would iron them out flat and make donkeys and dolls.' Marjorie Rathbone's husband Geoff was always the treasurer for National Saving Weeks. 'I did collecting, a penny a week for the Red Cross, as I pushed Peter round in his pushchair.' MR

✢ ✢ ✢   DR SCOTT AND THE CANTEEN

While recording our interviews, we were all struck by the frequent mention of Dr Gordon Scott, father of the present Dr Scott. Having been refused entry into the armed services because it was thought he would be more useful where he was, he did his utmost for the war effort from home. As well as looking after the health and welfare of the community, the name of Dr Scott was raised in many contexts – district councillor, secretary of War Savings for Chipping Norton Rural District, raising funds for use both at home and abroad, entertainment, and, particularly, the canteen.

In 1940 Dr Scott started a canteen in the YMCA Red Triangle hut on the present site of the entrance to Courtlands Road. The idea was to provide somewhere for evacuees and their mothers to go to give their foster-mothers a rest and to raise money for the founding of a Wychwoods Social Centre after the war, which sadly did not materialise. Only the cooks were paid; otherwise it was entirely staffed by volunteers.

Joan Hall worked there throughout the war and her sister, Mabel Souch, was one of the cooks.

Who actually organised it?

"Dr Scott did it all.

And he found people to volunteer and man it?

"Oh yes. He brought all the vegetables up before surgery in the morning out of his garden. That was for the lunches.

So it opened in the morning at 9 o'clock?

"9 o'clock and closed at 10 o'clock at night.

And how many people could be fed there?

"It must have been a lot because of course there were several soldiers and troops and they were nearly always in there. And lunchtimes there were quite a lot of children came up. There was nowhere else where you could get anything to eat. It was quite good. The evacuees, that was the main reason he started it, lunches for the evacuees. He always came in early in the morning and in the evening to see if there was anything we wanted.

In the mornings the troops came for coffee or whatever they wanted. And in the evenings they came for a cooked meal, eggs and bacon and things like that in the evening. Of course there were no school dinners at that time. So some of the schoolchildren used to come and lots of people who were working women. They came and got their husbands' and their lunch. And quite a lot of people, the district nurse and different people like that all used to come and have their meals. But we took it in shifts. Of course it was unpaid. There were two cooks for lunch [who] were paid. I laid the tables, that's the job I did at lunch time. That was 5 days a week, no week ends but as for the troops coming in in the morning and in the evening that was every day, Saturdays and Sundays and weekdays and all and that was all voluntary.

What sort of meal was served at lunchtime? Stew?

"Yes and fish.

Some sort of pudding?

"Yes. Rhubarb pudding. Done in a saucepan in a cloth, you know the sort that they used to do years ago. Yes they had some good meals. My sister was a good cook.

With the tea and coffee, were biscuits served?

"Yes, tea and coffee and biscuits. And we sold chocolates and cigarettes.

And how much did people pay?

JOAN HALL SITTING OUTSIDE
HER FATHER'S COTTAGE AT
THE BACK OF THE RED
HORSE, 1940.

" For their lunches they started off at sixpence each and then they decided that that didn't cover it – that was with a cup of tea. So then you paid a penny extra for a cup of tea. And that was all I can remember anybody paying.

And tea and coffee in the morning, that was a penny?

" Yes, that was it if they had it on its own. I know we did Sunday nights, my sister and I and a friend perhaps. And a cooked meal. Shall I tell you what I cooked one night? I'm always bragging to Jim about it. Ninety fried eggs and I never broke a yolk. That's all I have ever done in my life to make me stand out! That's what I always remember. That was for the soldiers.

Naturally Betty Scott also remembers her husband's involvement with the canteen. He would get supplies from anywhere he could and cajoled volunteers to help. Fruit and vegetables came from anyone who could be persuaded to give them.

" He did all the ordering and got the stuff from everywhere, and I had one night a week cooking chips and eggs for the men. And we tried to introduce tripe and onions because they were north country men and they loved tripe and onions but it didn't go down very well and I had to spend hours cooking the beastly stuff.

So where did all the produce come from, or don't we ask?

" We don't ask. I don't know where, I think he was allowed certain amounts of certificates [rations]. I think people helped with eggs and things and of course he would buy potatoes locally.

What did they cook on?

" Gas. Several times farmers gave him masses of rooks because they were such a nuisance and he used to get up at about 6 o'clock in the morning and cut the breasts out and I had to cook rook pie. But it didn't go down well. Some of them were a bit more adventuresome but felt that the fresh-done eggs and chips were best. BS

DOMESTIC LIFE ✝ ✝ ✝ ✝ ✝ ✝ ✝ ✝ ✝ ✝

Impressions of wartime in the Wychwoods are not so much dominated by the privations, restrictions and destruction of the time, as by the enormous contrast with life at the end of the twentieth century. Being able to afford to take advantage of the domestic electricity supply that had come to the Wychwoods in the early 1930s has probably been the most dramatic agent of change. Many cottages had no piped water, sewers, gas or electricity and few during the war had a refrigerator, a vacuum cleaner, a washing machine, or an electric cooker. Of course, there was no television; even radio was not yet universal.

Rose Burson was a young married woman in 1939.

Do you remember any special radio programmes that you listened to during World War Two?

" Never listened in.

You never listened in, you didn't have a radio?

" No. We never had any at home either. RB

Mary Barnes was a 12-year-old evacuee. 'I don't remember having a radio, actually, but I suppose there was a wireless'. Betty Scott, wife of the doctor, also could not remember listening to the radio. On the other hand, the radio was important to others. Betty Brown was 12 when war was declared. 'We always listened to the Vera Lynn programme on Sunday nights. They played requests for the forces and they played the national anthems of countries in the war. Also ITMA'.

And Vi Smith, who was 29 when war was declared, said:

" We had a radio which I used to have on quite a bit because it kept you in touch with what was going on and I remember Winston Churchill on the radio. VS

" At first it was head phones. And then you had bigger radios. It was nearly the start of the war before we had a radio. And it was as big a treat as the television today. JH

Colin Pearce described a weekly routine:.

"There was Rawlins' shop who sold bicycles. Charged your batteries up for your radio during the war. Always remember that we used to take it down every week. He had accumulators. Picked a new one up and took the old one down and paid your sixpence'.

A telephone, too was not yet general, although Mrs Scott was already tied to the house in order to answer it. The telephones in the Wychwoods were operated manually by Vi Smith's mother at 9 High Street, Shipton and 'manned' 24 hours a day, particularly for air-raid warnings. At Crows Castle, where Daphne Edginton moved in 1940 on her marriage, there was no telephone for some years after the war was over.

For many cooking was still on a solid-fuel range or oil stove.

" I cooked on a horrid black range with one oven each side actually but it never heated properly. It was supposed to heat the water as well but the bathroom was a mile away, not above it so to get a bath was quite a tricky business. We had to take some extra hot water up, buckets or something to get enough hot water to get in. DE

Shipton had its own gas works in Gas Lane and some houses had a supply. Mrs Scott had a gas cooker towards the end of the war, and remembered the difficulty of cooking even a tiny joint of meat on a Sunday because the gas pressure was so low.

Valerie Davies described the amenities of her home.

" The bathroom was downstairs with the copper in the room. I suppose we only had a bath once a week, and that was it.

And the loo was in the bathroom, was it?

" No, you went out the back door on the other side of the house and that was outside.

Did you have running water?

" Yes, cold.

And electricity?

"Yes and electricity.

What was the cooking done on?

"The original was an old black range, and we had that, then at some point Dad must have been doing up a house and the people gave him what we called a Triplex. It was a grate one side and it was enamelled and it looked better, and we had that with an oven. The everlasting memory is the Valor stove that would flicker a patch on the ceiling with the porridge bubbling in the morning. VD

Travelling was much curtailed by wartime but our interviewees still made trips to Oxford, mostly by train, or to Chipping Norton. Bicycles were the everyday means of transport and Peggy Coombes remembered cycling for miles.

As for entertainment, as Joan Hall said 'No, there was nothing on but you didn't notice because you had always been used to nothing on'. Dances were organised in the British Legion hall in Milton (close to the site of the present village hall) and in Shipton. There were film shows for children and also for the troops to which the locals went in the Red Triangle hut and Shipton Court. By 1945 Shipton cinema was open in Upper High Street, and it was not unusual for some to cycle every week to see a film at one of the two cinemas in Chipping Norton. Much of the local entertainment was home-made with fundraising in mind. Peggy Coombes summed up the problem. 'We were working pretty hard and pretty late most of the time'.

✠ ✠ ✠ ✠   WE WERE LUCKY OUT HERE

Food rationing affected people in the Wychwoods less severely than those living in the big towns. Gardens, allotments and the fields and hedgerows provided many supplements to the meagre if adequate rations.

"Well I think food began to get more restricted, although we were living in a country area and therefore almost able to live on what was produced around here. I mean we had our own garden, chickens and my husband used to shoot rabbits and he got on well with the farmers who he dealt with for the corn and that sort of thing and often came home with a little surprise, bit of meat that we treasured. VS

Vi Smith's husband became manager of Matthew's flour mill near the beginning of the war. Her daughter, Barbara Pearce, said 'I don't remember being anything but happy in my childhood. We were lucky out here. I don't remember being hungry'. The same thought was in Mary Barnes' mind when asked if there was enough to eat.

"We were very fortunate. Ivor had a big garden and he also used to shoot and fish and so we were very lucky. Rabbits. And they used to keep pigs down there with Mr Miles, Cocker Miles, they'd have one between them and then have another later on so we were very fortunate really. MB

Betty Brown's father was cowman at Little Hill Farm, Milton. She spoke in very similar tones. Unlike some she liked the dried egg.

"We had enough to eat as we had things from the farm. Rabbits. I haven't eaten one since. We cooked on an old-fashioned black range and on oil stoves. Can't recall any shortage of fuel. Mother was always bottling fruit and making jams. We kept a few chickens and Dad had extra cheese. We

DAPHNE EDGINTON SORTING EGGS IN THE KITCHEN AT CROW'S CASTLE FARM.

liked the dried egg; we used to mix it and do it like omelette. Tea was always short as mother was always making pots of tea, then borrowed from Lydiatts but that was always to be paid back. BB

But it was not all rabbit pie. For the Edgintons, deer could occasionally be added to the menu.

"Yes, well, we killed a pig of course as well so there was a bit of food there, lard and bacon and hams and Mr Davey got us what we hadn't got. DE

Where was the butcher's shop?

"Where Harman's is. And we were able to shoot deer. The army were in Barrington Park; they had taken over some of the Park of Mr Wingfield. They opened the gate and let the deer out and [they] are still in the wood. And one was down in the field of our barley one evening, just before Anthony was born, July 1941, and Bryan went down with a gun and shot it. Because we got no telephone we had to go down and fetch Mr Davey up to dress it and he hung it on the cherry tree outside and dressed it in the moonlight. We shot two more after that, we did rather well with the deer. They were nothing but a nuisance, getting in and frightening the sheep, which were in the fields in pens. So they were not good news to us, to see a deer out there. As I said there is not sheep penning now so that doesn't affect them. DE

Rose Burson also grew vegetables in her garden, bottled fruit and kept hens. She had a sad tale to tell about her attempt one year to make damson jam.

"I'll tell you something. We were allowed so much sugar for jam. I asked Mrs Edginton for some damsons because we all liked damson jam, to make some damson jam. Got the sugar. I had a notice come from Reading my Dad had had a fall. Would I go and see him. I went for the weekend. When I come back the damsons, sugar and everything had gone. RB

Where did it go?

"My mother-in-law had used them. She was always taking things. RB

The doctor's household experienced the same country fare, with the addition sometimes of goat's milk.

"We had chickens, we had rabbits, we had geese and we had a couple of goats but we weren't very successful at milking and every time we'd got a bowlful, one of them would put a foot in it and we'd have to throw it away. BS

Food was all bought locally, and Milton and Shipton each had a range of shops. Marjorie Rathbone's years of shopping with a ration book are

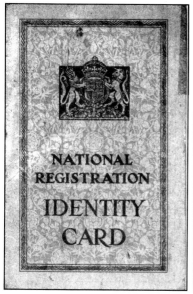

NATIONAL IDENTITY NUMBER: DZFA
FOR MILTON, 213 FOR HOUSEHOLD AND
2 FOR POSITION IN FAMILY.

imprinted on her mind.

"Even now, when I am out shopping, I can recall the order of the things that were on ration in the same order as they were in the rations books- tea, sugar, butter, marge, lard and cheese. I shopped mainly at the Post Office. We couldn't buy cake. We preserved fruit, mainly bottled, and we grew all our own vegetables. Horace Day kept a pig for us and we had to send it to Evesham for slaughter. We bought more land at the bottom of the garden so that we could keep chickens. Eric Meecham used to give us milk. There were extra rations for pregnant mothers, and then Peter had his own ration book which said Rathbone Baby, as we hadn't given him a name at the time. MR

And Joan Hall described the meat ration. 'If you had a tin of corned beef, you couldn't have meat that weekend, because it just did for one ration. One tin of corned beef. It was quite a treat to get corned beef in those days'.

Food was a constant preoccupation for any housewife during the war. Not much came in convenient tins and packs and much time was taken up with growing, digging, washing and preparing vegetables and fruit. Rationing did not end in 1945 and shortages of food continued to dominate life for years after peace was made. 'Obviously for Mother it must have been difficult, but we weren't used to exotic food or anything different,' commented Valerie Davis.

Daphne Edginton was living at Crows Castle with her husband and young family and she did have to provide some things then considered 'more exotic'. Along with coping with farming and motherhood, Daphne had a long line of prisoners of war working on the farm. 'So I had to provide their food of course. I had to get used to cooking macaroni for the Italians and Germans who seemed to have all sorts of things like that'.

The difficulties and restrictions might not be tackled so resourcefully now.

WORK FOR WOMEN OUTSIDE THE HOME

With the outbreak of war, girls were encouraged to take some sort of employment helpful to the war effort with registration for National Service beginning at 18 years by December 1941. Many took over occupations previously dominated by men. Irene Carpenter, Dorothy Treweeke and Peggy Coombes were all sent to work here as Land Army girls (and ended up finding husbands too).

Irene Carpenter née Groom was born in Burton on Trent on 25 October, 1925. She joined the Women's Land Army in 1943, leaving her job in an arts and craft studio. She spent part of the war at Shipton Court Farm where she worked with the herd of Jersey cows owned by Mrs Hall. The milk was sent to Oxford.

"I got the papers and Dad had to sign them because I was too young and then went to Reace Heath Agricultural College in Nantwich. It was a quick course, a little bit of everything, horses, pigs, butter-making, hand and machine milking and a little bit of horticulture. I was sent down to a farm round the Iffley area outside Oxford. I did the milking but then they put me in the dairy which was very heavy work because we did have these seventeen and half gallon churns which you had to tip to get the milk out to put it in the cooler. I didn't like it very much; I was half starved. Then I went to Mrs Hall's to do the milking. She lived in Mawles Lane but most of the girls were billeted in Springhill Cottages. The farm was on the other side of the road, Home Farm Close now. I should imagine it was about 80 milkers, lovely little cows. We very often used to walk them up to the top of the Swinbrook Road crossroads, to graze up there and of course somebody had to stay with them because you had to go round to see they didn't eat too much and 'blow'. LC

Living conditions were basic but while at Shipton she had to surrender her ration book in exchange for having all her food provided and served at the bothy in the stables at Shipton Court.

" Money was taken for our keep, and I think it was about 7s 6d we had left, but we was a happy lot, we didn't fall out much. LC

Irene later moved to farms at Glympton and Wilcote. She had, however, met her future husband, Ramsey Carpenter, at the Red Horse while working in Shipton and they married at St Mary the Virgin Church, Shipton in 1946.

Dorothy Treweeke née Parr left her office job in Cleckheaton near Bradford at the age of seventeen and joined the Women's Land Army as her parents refused to sign the forms for her to join the WAAF. Her first job after training in Northampton was on Earl Spencer's farms potato-picking. She was there for eighteen months and then went on to work in the cowsheds and then looking after the calves, pigs and chickens on other

IRENE CARPENTER (ABOVE) AND (RIGHT) IN 1943 WHILE WORKING AT IFFLEY BEFORE COMING TO MRS HALL AT SHIPTON.

farms. However Dorothy's mother was taken ill and she had to return home. By September 1944 she was keen to get away again.

" So I asked for a transfer and was sent to Hill Crest, to work for Norman's father. Up the Bruern Road they lived. I had come to drive the tractor. He had chickens; he used to rear them and sell the eggs or incubate the eggs and when the chicks were so many days old, we used to take them down to Shipton Station and send them to different people because they were a pedigree - I can't remember – Plymouth Rock, I think. I was helping with those in the morning and then I used to go up to Foxholes and do the tractor-driving, ploughing and harrowing. He rented it from Miss Bailey. Norman's father taught me how to drive, yes in Foxholes, I never had a driving test. He showed me what to do and I just drove round and round the field and then one day he said, 'Do you think you could manage to go down home and get something?' and I did. But you see there was nothing on the roads in those days and you didn't meet anybody because the private cars you couldn't get petrol for, it was only the farmers. They were quite hard times really, the haymaking was one and the threshing, when we threshed you used to get caught up with the sheaves, they used to scratch your arms, it was quite heavy really. But no, I really enjoyed it. DT

After the war she married Mr Treweeke's son Norman and they took over the milkround from Mr Davis.

Peggy Coombes was living on the outskirts of Bristol when war was declared.

" I was working in a drawing office at the Bristol Aeroplane Company at Filton. Very interesting work but it did not really satisfy me in some way or other. So when I had the chance to join the Land Army I jumped at it. Actually I had an awful job to get out because it was a protected occupation. But I made myself such a nuisance that they let me go. At the beginning we were very lucky, we went to college so we weren't absolutely ignorant when we got to the farms like some of them were. This was in July 1940, about six weeks but it was very intensive. We did a bit of everything – over 60 of us, all sorts and nationalities. I went to Somerset to start with. We were given one pair of dungarees and one pair of breeches and one shirt to start with and you had to give up coupons for anything else you wanted. So when you wanted your breeches washed you had to wear either your own slacks or skirt. I remember the first winter I had chilblains on my knees. We were paid 28s a week and we had to give up 14s to the farmer's wife for our keep and if we did overtime we were paid 7d an hour. And the first farm I went to I started by washing the cows at half past five in the morning, worked until half past 7 at night, clearing up the dairy after they had bottled the milk and when I asked for my 7d overtime I was told to find another job. This was a very large dairy, over 150 cows. I suppose it was about 18 months altogether that I was dairying. And then the girl I joined with who lives locally as well [Mrs Griffin at Fifield] she was on an arable

DOROTHY TREWEEKE IN HER LAND ARMY UNIFORM IN 1942 (LEFT) AND (BELOW) ON A TRACTOR OUTSIDE HILL CREST, BRUERN ROAD, IN 1944 WHERE SHE WORKED FOR MR TREWEEKE.

farm and her farmer wanted another girl. So I came to Gloucestershire and ended up at Gawcombe. Tetbury was all horse, ploughing with three horses but at Gawcombe it was tractors. I was not a tractor driver - [I would] ride the drill, that sort of thing, harvest, hay making. I think farming is the most satisfying job you can possibly have; you see the end results. PC

Peggy developed tonsillitis and had to leave the Land Army. She stayed on in Shipton and worked in the office at the F.W.P. Matthew's mill. Like the other land army girls we interviewed who came to the Wychwoods area to work, she too met her future husband, Bob Coombes, here, at a dance organised by Dr Scott in the Beaconsfield Hall after the village fete.

These three Land Army girls came to the Wychwoods. For Dorothy Harrison, born in Ascott in 1924, war service took her out of the area.

" Father worked at No 8 MU [Maintenance Unit] at Little Rissington. He even helped to build it. They had a bus but, at first, he had to cycle there. He stayed there until he stopped work. He even did Home Guard duties there instead of back in the Ascott platoon.

After school in Ascott, Dorothy had started work at 14. She was filled with enthusiasm at the prospect of war.

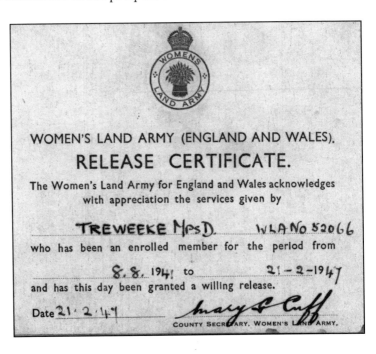

WOMEN'S LAND ARMY (ENGLAND AND WALES).

RELEASE CERTIFICATE.

The Women's Land Army for England and Wales acknowledges with appreciation the services given by

TREWEEKE Mrs D.   WLA No 52066

who has been an enrolled member for the period from

8. 8. 1941 to   21-2-1947

and has this day been granted a willing release.

Date 21· 2 ·47   mary P Cuff

COUNTY SECRETARY, WOMEN'S LAND ARMY.

PEGGY COOMBES RIDING THE DRILL AT GAWCOMBE IN 1943

"I was delighted. Honestly. I only wanted the war to go on long enough to join up – in the RAF. When the war began I was working at Yew Tree Farm, next door doing chickens and eggs and things like that. That's why when I joined up he said, 'It's a reserved occupation'. He said that he had to sign a paper [to secure release] and he said he didn't know [if he would]. I said, 'Well, if you won't sign I won't work'. I went to New Inn Hall Street in Oxford in 1942. Then I was posted to Innsworth Lane, Gloucester for square bashing and then came the hardest two years of my life. I did five years in the WAAF and the last three were a complete joy after the first two as a barrage-balloon operator and that was no job for a woman, believe you me. On the northeast coast above the Newcastle shipyards. We used to get bombed every night and if you didn't get bombed there was a storm raging all night, and you pulled all night to hold the balloon in position. A terrible thing for a girl to do, it was very hard. On the northeast coast the balloons either got shot down or a storm ripped them off.

At 18 I was a corporal in charge of a balloon site in the East End of London and because we would not fly balloons as they were trying out other devices for a month, no shops would serve us and nobody would speak to us.

AIRCRAFT FITTER
(ENGINES) DOROTHY
HARRISON, AT RAF
CROUGHTON IN 1944. SHE
IS TO THE RIGHT OF
ENGINE IN THE BACK ROW,
SECOND FROM THE LEFT.

We were very close to people – sometimes stationed in someone's garden, wherever the pattern was needed. On one occasion the girl next to me was killed by shrapnel when on duty in the East End. I was also on a site in the moat of the Tower of London. Then after the bombing let up they did not need so many balloons so I re-mustered as an aircraft engine fitter. At the end of 1943 1 went to St Athan, South Wales. Then I was posted to RAF Croughton as an aircraft fitter and after 3 years to RAF Ternhill in Shropshire. After five years in the WAAF I went to Birmingham [to be demobbed] and then back to Ascott.

In 1947 she married Sergeant Pilot Al Harrison, and after a working life with the Metropolitan Police, they returned to the Wychwoods, to Milton, in 1980.

Some local girls worked at RAF Little Rissington. Betty Brown née Duester, born at Kingham Hill in 1927, moved to the cottage at the end of Frog Lane aged three when her father was cowman at Lower Farm, Upper Milton. Later the family moved to a cottage at the far end of The Square when he became cowman at Little Hill Farm. From here Betty attended Milton school and then Burford Council school. She began in domestic service for Brigadier General Kirby at Heath House, Lyneham

BETTY BROWN (CENTRE) AT NO 8 MU LITTLE RISSINGTON IN FRONT OF AN ASSEMBLED HOTSPUR GLIDER, USED FOR TRAINING GLIDER PILOTS.

Road, and then worked for a time at The Swan, Minster Lovell. By then the war had started and her only brother, John, had been called up. Rather than going away from home too, Betty went to work at No 8 Maintenance Unit, RAF Little Rissington at the age of 16.

"I was at the top hangar on the big Horsa gliders, the ones that took the troops, and then I moved to the bottom hangar. Here I worked on Spitfires that were sent to Malta. We only worked day shifts but when we were doing the Spitfires we had to work three Sunday shifts to get them ready. We did the modifications on them before they went back into use. Some American Dakotas came to collect some of the small Hotspur gliders. I worked on those as well. We went to work by airforce bus, all camouflaged. They went round all the villages. The men were riggers and fitters. We did the sort of rough work, putting on patches etc. I am not sure if we dealt with crashed planes but they had a field of planes no longer in use, Wellington bombers. There were meals in the NAAFI but I always took sandwiches. We wore overalls as we were climbing all over the aircraft. BB

While at RAF Little Rissington Betty met Addy Brown who had been directed here from his native northeast of England. They were married in Milton in 1946 where Betty still lives.

Brenda Bishop née Brewerton also worked at No 8 MU at RAF Little Rissington. Born near Coventry, at 15 she came to live with her grandmother and new husband, Wycliffe Dore, in Spring Cottage beyond the end of Green Lane. After her grandmother died in 1938, Brenda lodged with Mrs Agnes Earley and worked as a van-driver delivering milk for Poplar Farm, Milton. She passed her goods vehicle driving test, so women were beginning to go into such occupations even before the necessities of wartime made it more common.

" As I was working for Mr Wells at Poplar Farm I stayed on till the war got under way. I delivered milk by van to all the villages but lived with Agnes Earley when Ken, her husband went to war work. Later I went to Little Rissington No 8 MU [maintenance unit] as an MT [motor transport] driver; I am not sure of the date that I started. As there were only one or two people working at 8 MU at that time we went together with Roland who was given enough petrol to get to work. There were already two other female drivers working there, one to drive the test pilots and the other the top foreman. I was a heavy-duty driver so had a truck and tractor to drive as was needed, the tractor to tow planes and the truck to haul equipment and personnel. Soon others from around the three Wychwoods were getting work at 8 MU enough to run a bus to take us back and forth, and headquarters decided to take me off site and give me the CO's car at headquarters, also a van to drive when needed for trips away from camp, London, Wales and in between. This was what I enjoyed most. There were happy times and sad ones, like a plane crashing on the equipment store. It was at night after a raid and on its way back to base. So we all went ahead with our jobs until the war ended. There were quite a few MT drivers, about six women, the rest were men. I was just helping out the men. BrB

In her spare time she was busy with the Girl Guides, keep-fit and amateur dramatics and later she served on the committees of the Comforts Fund and WI. In December 1946, Brenda left England for the United States where she now lives in Florida.

Cicely Miller née Tibbitts was born in Maestag, South Wales in 1921 and came to the Wychwoods in 1932. Her father, gassed in the First World War, had gone to South Wales to find work. With difficult times in Wales her father then moved to Aylesbury to work in a brewery.

Following an illness attributed to wartime gassing, it was suggested he return to his native village of Milton. The family moved into 4 Pear Tree Close in 1931, the last of those new council houses to be occupied. Cis attended Burford Council school and then began work at Mrs Davis' shop at London House, High Street, Milton. At the outbreak of war, she helped her widowed mother with evacuees and then she was called up for National Service.

" In the second year of the war, when I was 20, I was called up. So I went from Mrs Davis' to the British Aluminium Company at Banbury. I think that I went down to Shipton to catch the bus, then lodged in Banbury during the week and then came home at weekends – if we weren't working weekends.

After appendicitis Cis was unable to lift the heavy sheets of metal onto the machine so she was re-directed to Witney where De Havilands repaired crashed aircraft. In the early war years these were mainly Tiger Moths, an early training plane, but as the war progressed they repaired Spitfires and Hurricanes, the vital fighter planes.

" At first I was in the stores and then moved to the stores' office. I stayed at De Havilands to the end of the war. We worked six days a week, sometimes seven. I left Milton on the early bus which was utility with wooden slatted

CIS TIBBITTS (RIGHT) AND MRS MILLEN FROM MILTON (LEFT) AT DE HAVILANDS WITNEY.

seats. It left Milton at 6.15am to arrive at Witney at 7.30am as we went all round the villages, Chadlington, Charlbury and the rest of them.

In her spare time she was in the Guides as well as being Brown Owl, amateur dramatics, keep-fit, the Comforts Fund and the Wychwood choir, as well as a youthful member of the Wychwoods British Legion and Women's Institute. At De Havilands she met John Miller who had been directed there from Hampshire. They were married in 1948 and made their home at 4 Pear Tree Close where they still live.

THE EFFECTS OF WAR ✝ ✝ ✝ ✝ ✝ ✝ ✝

Our interviewees showed amazingly little emotion when talking about the events of the war. Frightening incidents were described matter-of-factly with no great show of fear, anger or hatred. There was only one 'terrified'. Expressions used of events were 'worried', 'a little worried' 'frigid', 'terrible'. Daphne Edginton described what happened to her the morning after war was declared. Her honest description of crying was one of two mentions of tears in the interviews.

"I got up very early in the morning – I was still at home, of course, at Churchill Heath, and I got the wireless on and the first thing I heard the Athenian ship was sunk in the Atlantic. I burst into tears. I don't often burst into tears but I did that morning. It really brought it home to us what was happening. And one of our friends, a neighbouring farmer, had just been on it to America for a tour, an agricultural tour of America - the very ship. We couldn't believe it. DE

She also described the advent and prolonged stay of two of the many wartime guests at Churchill Heath. They were 'terrified' by war.

"A daughter brought her mother up from Hythe, Kent because they were terrified. This mother was nearly 90, totally deaf, and the daughter put her in the car with a few bits of their prized belongings, silver and jewellery, and came to the White Hart in Chipping Norton. We knew the proprietor of the White Hart there quite well and they landed there. They wanted to get out of the hotel into somebody's house so we had them. My mother would have anybody! So, they had a bedroom and the dining room. We'd still got the breakfast room and the kitchen. And, believe it or not, in 1941 the daughter died of Hodgkins disease before the mother, so here we were left with the mother, this old lady, deaf as a post. DE

Joan Hall, whose father was a signalman at Bruern railway crossing and whose mother had died several years before the war, described the dark, lonely nights at the height of the bombing.

Presumably the war changed things for your father workwise? The number of trains must have increased.

"Actually that was our biggest worry. At home, with my sister who was a year older than me and my other sister who was five years younger, of course my dad had to work nights and we were afraid. He was in the signal box and the stairs came up outside at Bruern and of course we were worried at home in case he got bombed being on the railway line and he was worried in case we did at home. JH

"Father did get a little worried about German planes going over as he had one brother in Birmingham and another in Coventry and there were frequent raids there. Father went walking at night, watching the lights and the lights of fires in the sky. BB

What about the first siren or air raid warning?

"Well, as I say, I was in Chipping Norton at the time. It must have been September or October 1939. I was living there at that time and the warning went and it was the first time ever and we all went down the lower floor and sat feeling absolutely frigid. DE

The bombing of Coventry was a consistent memory.

"Yes, when that happened we wondered what on earth was happening by the number of planes that were coming over and we went in the car up to the Merrymouth up the road and there we could see these lights flashing and sparks flying and we found it was Coventry the next day. We didn't think you could see it from that distance, Just shows how it shows up in the darkness and how high the sparks come up - the explosions. DE

"I can remember when Coventry was bombed, that was a very bad night, yes. We were coming home with the Baptist minister's wife – she used to run a club and I used to go there – and when we were coming home that particular night, you could see the red light on the horizon and the glow of the fire and that and you could hear the planes going droning over, the Germans, I can remember that very well. MB

"Yes, when Coventry was blitzed, the one big night they did it, we went up on, dozens of us, I don't know how we come together, went up to the bridge up here and you could see Coventry being - you could see all the fires from Coventry in the sky. It really lit the sky up. It was terrible because by that time lots of soldiers had got up there and seen and a lot of them came from

Coventry and it must have been awful for them. We always felt sorry for them that night because it was absolutely terrific. JH

As this project has been concerned with women in the Wychwoods during the Second World War, the menfolk and those serving in the armed forces have only been mentioned in passing, but were often, or perhaps always, in the women's minds. On the declaration of war, many must have shared Vi Smith's apprehension:

Was it a dramatic event?

"Well of course I was naturally worried whether my husband would have to go, but as he was in food processing he was exempt. It was necessary for him to help to run the mill so fortunately he didn't have to go. I mean when the Second World War started they said, 'Oh, it won't last many weeks' and look at it. VS

Six years later, when peace in Europe was made on 8 May 1945, at least 200 men and women from Ascott, Milton and Lyneham, and Shipton had at some time been on active service. This was a significant proportion of the men and women of the villages, which altogether had a population of under 2000 in 1931. Most of their names have been gathered from the

THE WEDDING OF DAPHNE AND BRYAN EDGINTON IN 1940 WITH BRYAN'S BROTHER RALPH AND DAPHNE'S SISTERS, VIVIENNE (LEFT) AND MONICA (RIGHT).

records of the Comforts Fund and from the record in Ascott's Tiddy Hall compiled by Eric Moss, which records Dorothy Harrison as the only woman from Ascott on Active Service. Most of the 200 survived the war having served in many parts of the world. Even so it must have been a worry for all those left behind in the Wychwoods, especially for the four families whose menfolk were posted as 'Missing', but later turned up as Prisoners of War.

But lives were lost as the War Memorials record, four from Ascott, five from Milton, Bruern and Lyneham and eight from Shipton. From these names, no child lost a father and only one woman lost her husband. All will be remembered. During the war years local burials included those who had been on Active Service, evacuated persons, victims of road accidents and persons of all ages from two and half months to 94 years. With no known grave is May Muriel Clifford from Shipton who lost her life through enemy action on the *Gloucester Castle* in 1942 on her way to work as a missionary in Southern Africa.

"I think the stress was worse than anything else really. I mean, I know the people that were in the bombed areas had, but there was also a lot of stress in the village with people going to war, losing people and you wondering who was next. We knew people more intimately in those days and therefore if anybody had bereavement you sort of felt it for them. VS

"Well, my brother was in the army, Tony, and my next one, Peter, was in the merchant navy. He was travelling all over the place and he never heard a depth charge or saw anything. He came through and brought the King of Greece back from South Africa or somewhere to England and they didn't see anything. He didn't go in a convoy. Their ships were too fast. DE

So he had it a lot easier than Tony then?

"Yes. Tony was landed on the North African beaches and went all along there and across to Sicily up to the Battle of Monte Cassino and ended up in Vienna. He looked a total wreck when he came home and he could no longer go and work in the City of London and he came back on to the land into the fresh air. Different personality. DE

Joan Hall recalled the effect that working in a munitions factory had on her brother.

"One of my brothers was sent, they were sent, several of them, to ammunition work in Southampton and do you know what? They were worse than if they had been at war. It made real wrecks of them. They were allowed to come home once a fortnight for the weekend and they were absolutely...they lost their hair and they were so thin, they were bombed so much because they bombed the ammunition works and of course that was terrible. JH

Most of those who had been evacuated here officially or otherwise returned to the cities. Those who had served with the armed forces returned home more slowly. Some wartime relationships ended in tragedy but many flourished.

It is right to end with the hopefulness of wartime and immediate post-war marriages, and the victory celebrations. Wartime weddings were described by our interviewees with delight and satisfaction, tinged with poignancy. It was as if the brides took special pride in having surmounted the scarcity of material, sugar, petrol and time to produce a memorable occasion. Daphne Edginton and Joan Hall described their wartime weddings. Daphne's was similar to her brother, Dick's.

"We just had the service at Churchill Church and had tea in the drawing room and we left about half past four and we went to Ledbury, then on to Wales. We had petrol in the tank. Because that seemed the safest place to go at that time, 1940. But we then heard the bombs dropping on Cardiff so we hurriedly came back to the Cotswolds. Yes, that wasn't much fun. DE

"We got married in 1941. Jim was stationed in England and then he had to go abroad and we got married. We had prepared to get married and we had made all the bridesmaids' clothes and things like that. And then he had to go abroad in a rush so we got married in May instead of July. He came home on a Thursday and I said 'Oh, lovely, are you home for the weekend?' and he said 'No, I have to go back on Saturday', and so we - he met me off the train, I'd been to Oxford, and he told me so we immediately went in to Witney and got a license and my sister got the wedding ring in Oxford. She chose the wedding ring and that was that, wasn't it? But when it came to buying the wedding cake, they weren't icing wedding cakes. They were cardboard, the main of them, and it looked like a wedding cake. But we were lucky, we got a wedding cake. And I had got my wedding dress, by the way, which was £8. Mind, that was a lot of money then. He was leaving from Kingham Station and I went to Kingham in my wedding dress to see him off and I didn't see him for four and a half years then. JH

Joan Hall and her husband Jim wrote to each other every day during those four and a half years that he was away in service. At one point he was missing for six months and Joan's efforts to find him were aided by the vicar, Rev. Windsor Cundell. Even the Air Force did not knew his whereabouts. Amazingly, communication suddenly resumed. Joan

JOAN HALL IN HER WEDDING DRESS TAKEN A WEEK OR TWO AFTER HER WEDDING IN MAY 1941 AS NO PHOTOGRAPHS COULD BE TAKEN ON THE DAY. BY THEN HER BOUQUET OF CARNATIONS HAD FADED SO SHE HOLDS GARDEN FLOWERS.

described this event in her usual understated style.

"Yes, and I'll tell you they were so kind, Miss Coombes, Jessie. During the peacetime we had two deliveries, one about 2 o'clock in the afternoon and one about 8 o'clock in the morning. And with the war on we only had one delivery. And one afternoon she came to me, she said 'Joan', she said, 'You've got a letter from Jim come this afternoon and so we thought we wouldn't leave it for you to worry until tomorrow morning so we are delivering it this afternoon'. I thought that was nice of them and Jim had got an old auntie who had brought him up because his mother had died when he was born and he had an auntie that brought him up and I was able to let her know. She got an extra night's sleep because I was able to let her know. I thought it was so nice of Miss Coombes because they only did the thing that was right and if the Post Office said they could only deliver the one a day, they could only deliver one a day. Then she came that afternoon and brought that letter. People were so kind. JH

Betty Brown remembered the VE Day celebrations at RAF Little Rissington. 'We heard in the morning. We had a dance band so we celebrated in the canteen. There were airmen there who went round cutting the ends off each other's ties. Everyone went crazy.' A year later she married Addy Brown whom she had met at Rissington.

"We were married in Milton Church in 1946. I had a white wedding as someone had given me a book of clothing coupons so I was able to buy a white wedding dress. But, of course, everything was short. We had dockets for [utility] furniture and, as food was short, we only had 30 guests at the reception in the British Legion hall with sausage rolls and sandwiches and two bottles of sherry. BB

MILTON FANCY DRESS PARTY ON VICTORY THANKSGIVING DAY 8 JUNE 1946

Mary Barnes, evacuated here as an eleven-year-old 'for a fortnight's holiday', decided to stay on when her mother returned to London. She had been saving for her marriage to Leslie Barnes. She had borrowed a wedding dress from her aunt.

Do you remember the Red Triangle hut at Shipton?

"Yes, that's where I had my wedding reception, there on 23 June. I had been working at the shop and, of course, everything was on ration and I'd been saving all these things up, jellies and that sort of thing. And it was such a hot day, I can remember, and all the jellies melted. It was corrugated iron.

Betty Scott has a particular memory of the end of the war.

"When the troops came back and grocer's chap came to take an order at the back door he enthusiastically held out his hand to be shaken and said 'It's so nice to see old faces, Mrs Scott.' It made me feel about 106. BS

+ + + + + + + + + + + +

As the twentieth century ends, it is worth a moment to consider the essential value of the Wychwood women who gave so much in World War Two, as surely as their menfolk did. They are the unsung heroines of the Wychwoods.